THE SOUL'S DESIRE

THE SOUL'S DESIRE

ADITI MISHRA

Made with ❤ on the Notion Press Platform
www.notionpress.com

To Lord Krishna, Deepti, Mum and Dad.

Dear Kanhaji, without you it would'nt have been possible for me to be able to do this. Dear Deepti, without you I wouldn't have realised that I write goood :) Thanks for all the appreciation. My dearest mom, thankyou for telling me to try my best always and daddy thankyou for becoming my support. I love you all. You're all source of my motivation.

Contents

Yes, I Do

Poem 3: For All Loved Ones

Me...

And...

Man...

Dear Father...

Dear Mom...

The Home...

Tell Me...

Dear Night ,

"?"

The World From My Window

A Lot Vs Little

It's Better...

If You...

Dearest Teacher,

Dear Grief...

An Elder Daughter...

Dear Monsoon...

Accepting The Truth

Hurt...

Contents

Preface

Entering into the most mysterious phase of my life or hitting puberty, changed my life severly. From a girl with very less or no acquaintances whom I misunderstood as friend to a girl having real friends. From a girl with no emotions to an ocean of emotions inside. From not leaving the home to the urge of coming late. From a girl of pure logic to a girl of emotions. From a stone-hearted to a very sensitive one. These poems are all a collection which I wrote in my transition phase. With chapters created to make a bundle of having similar ones.

Acknowledgements

I wish to express my gratitude to each and everyone who's reading or even not reading this book. Thanks to the lord for giving me this beautiful life in human form. To my parents for loving me unconditionally and for my upbringing. To my sister who is the best sibling I could ever have. To my lovely teacher for whom I wrote my first poem. Only beacuse of her I entered to this beautiful world of writing. To my friends who have been there for me always. To my bestie who held me through each and every up and down. To all the people who made my feelings go so wild that it compelled me to knit them into words. To everyone who had their faith in me even I didn't and to everyone for existing.

Prologue

There's a girl in her teens , extremely sensitive. She thinks thas it is her soul's desire to write , that's why she justifies her book title as the "The Soul's Desire". She is extremely happy or sad , she finds it very difficult to be in between but she applies an antiseptic lotion on herself, called "TIME" and heals. Throughout her journey all her experiences she has tried to express them in poems.

1. Chapter 1: The First Poem My Journey from

Attached Note : Below is the first ever poem of mine which I wrote for my favourite teacher. She has an irreplacable and a very special place in my heart. Hope you find it beautiful.

Darkness to a room full of light

Hating Sanskrit to love it

Copying work at last moment to always complete work

Hating sanskrit teacher to love you

Neglecting it to curiosity

Hating sanskrit period to being eagerly excited for it

Finding excuses to miss sanskrit period to hate to miss it

From rote to being practical

This all my journey is just because of you,

There's a lot to say but exist words are a few.

Well, I can write a book on you,

But still that book will not fully complete you.

13ᵗʰ of Feb, When I firstly realised that for me, who are you.

There are a lot of teachers, but no one as you.

I know that I haven't seen the world yet,

But for me the whole world is in you.

Lots of improvements in me, the reason is you.

What I am today is just because of you.

I like your everything, from teaching to taking test,

Nobody can be perfect, what you're the best.
In future, I'll meet to many other teachers,
But I can never forget you
Even the whole life is not sufficient to describe you.
Again this all my journey is just because of you.
Time was less, had to finish it early
but still this poem can be extended endlessly.

2. Chapter 2: The Transition

I'm not Heartless

Why after so much efforts ,
My result seems effortless ?
Why after each try ,
the result is worthless ?
Why after results ,
my effort seems worthless ?
Each of my effort , to bring smile on the faces ,
is going worthless ?
I love them , but only telling is'nt sufficient
and proving myself is useless.
My feelings and words always mismatch
and every effort to match them is going result less.
I wish I could speak , what I feel ,
then I wouldn't have seen their faces smile less.
I'm not what I look ,
I'm not careless.
Though it may look like ,
but I'm not heart less.

You won't see me crying , You won't see me enjoying.
You'll see me rude , angry , aggressive and frustrating.
But let me tell you my dear ones..
I'm not emotion less.
It's difficult to see the inner me , because I'm surrounded by circumstances,
But still if you can see the inner me , I would be speechless.
I'm clear as a crystal,
Softer than a bristle.
Harder than a diamond,
More precised than an almond.
I'm a puzzled thread ,
I'm a mysterical head.
Trying to move ahead,
By saying to me , whatever happened... Just forget.
I'm a half read book,
Judged by the outer look.
To read it , once you took,
Still floating as a brook.

Yes, I Do

Attached Note : Ever felt like you love someone immensely but they turn out to accompany you for just their advantage ? But still not able to leave them ? I've got something you could relate to.

Yes, I wait sometimes for you to be unhappy,

Yes, I wait sometimes for your situations to become unhandy,

Yes, I wait sometimes for you to have bad days,

Yes, I wait sometimes for you to be out of ways,

Yes, I wait for your smile to turn into frown,

Yes, I wait for your tears to roll down...

I wait for all these, not because I hate you, not because I don't like your smile.

I wait and yes it's true, so that you would remember me, ask for help and I'll.

People need time to talk, you need reason.

Whenever you remember me, I know it's for a reason.

Only if you could talk unreasonably, then I would not wait unnecessarily.

Poem 3: For all loved ones

Don't let your tears fall , I'm not there to wipe them up.

Don't let your smile fade away , I'm not there to cheer you up.

Don't skip your food , I'm not there to feed you up.

Sleep on time , I'm not there to caress your head .

And don't forget the blanket , I'm not there to put it up.

Don't be tired , I'm not there to give you rest.

Don't be angry , I'm not there to listen you up.

Don't let yourself get wounded , I'm not there to heal you up.

Don't burden yourself , I'm not there to help you in lifting it up.

Don't let your emotions overflow , I'm not there for the extra to catch it up.

It's difficult , I know.

Thinking after a certain extent what to do?

When it's not possible what all I said.

When you feel like your tears have to shed.

When you feel the capacity is over of the Mug.

Just come to me with a tight hug.

Such extreme condition whenever you spot.

In my presence , replace all the "don'ts" with "Do"s , "There"s with "Here"s

add Since before every I and vanish all the 'not's.

It'll become :

Do let your tears fall , Since I'm here to wipe them up.

Do let your smile fade away , Since I'm here to cheer you up.

Do skip your food , Since I'm here to feed you up.

Even if you Sleep on time , I'm here to caress your head .

And do forget the blanket ,Since I'm here to put it up.

Do get tired , Since I'm here to give you rest.

Do get angry , Since I'm here to listen you up.

Do let yourself get wounded , Since I'm here to heal you up.

Do burden yourself , Since I'm here to help you in lifting it up.

Do let your emotions overflow , Since I'm here for the extra to catch it up.

Me...

I have a lot to say,

But not the courage.

I feel a lot ,

But can't express.

Come and feel me , you'll know

How much I supress (my feelings).

I'm rude from outside,

But I'm soft , when you peek inside.

I... Can motivate you

Will show , that I don't need you.

But ask from my heart ,

How much do I need you.

Motivation is what.. I also need

Not to succeed..

But to get me .

When I say , you're nothing to me

You mean a lot to me!...

And...

And you'll think you're the happiest person ever.

With whom, even after having one less dose of food , you'll grow.

You'll feel like the pale blue day, has met the sun, to make it coloured &
beautiful.

Totally unaware of the beauty of the moon.

You'll feel like the heaven is here

like having all the happiness around there.

And then suddenly , all white clouds would disappear,

making the day dull & dark, like on a clean cotton sheet a huge black mark.

You'll be shattered into pieces in no time.

Your countless infinite pieces will scatter themselves,

as the colours of the rainbow.

May be, more beautiful than that,

but sharper than any glass.

Gorgeous to look but painful to touch.

Your smile would fade just as such.

And here you'll realise, the sun has gone.

You would be sad, but more of shocked.

Unable to digest whatever happened.

After a span you'll digest.

Will think it was a life's test.

You'll realise it was not about the bad or the good.

It was that it was a sun, made for the day.

And you were unaware that you are the night, ignoring all the stars.

Time would be the antiseptic you would apply,

which would heal all the wound.

And the night sky, would meet the beautiful moon.

Man…

A man hurt me, but a man consolidated me too.

A man left me, but a man always had my back.

A man was the reason of my tears, but a man wiped those tears too.

When it was dark, I was afraid because of a man but a man assisted me safely in that too.

People say that men don't cry but I have seen him crying helplessly.

People say men are emotion less but I've seen him sensitive.

World says a lot to me to make some stereotypes about you, but I never listen.

I want you to know that I love you and will always.

Don't allow the perception of society to stop you from anything.

Don't know about society but I'll love you for everything.

You cry, or speak soft. Earn money or do the household chores.

Become a responsible son, or do what you want leaving the responsibilities on your sister shoulders.

Be inactive physically, or be non muscular.

Be what you want, let the world say you peculiar.

Because I love you for your heart and soul.

Even if I fail to show, but I don't judge if you don't fit this societal MEN'S bowl.

Why Should You?

There are no good or bad men or women, there are just humans and devils.

Dear Father...

I love all my friends, but through this dare ,

You wanted to know , who's in trend.

Let me tell you my dear friend ,

Whoever he is , he pushed me ahead.

Given me courage, when I was sad.

He guided me , He motivated me , when I was hopeless as dead.

He scolded me , he taught me ,

He made me fly like a bird.

He knew my worst , he knew my best.

He taught me how to give , the life's test.

He let me fly , by taking all the burden on his head.

And my effort to pay off , wouldn't be great.

Yes , my dear friend,

He's nobody other , but my beloved Dad.

Dear Mom...

My dear mother ,

You can't be compared with any other.

You gave me birth ,

a chance to live on this Earth.

You spent sleepless nights,

So that I could sleep.

Which this world , cannot

understand.

You helped me , You taught me.

You fed me , You served me.

Describing you & your love

in just words.

Would be of no use , just useless.

Thanking you , is like lighting a lamp , in front of a sun.

You taught me how to learn.

You taught me why to earn? (respect and prestige)

You made me what I am,

Thank-you my mother , for all that you've done.

The Home...

The home is where, stays the heart...

Where this beautiful journey , known as the life starts.

Lots of memories and your art,

From where you can have , a peek of the past.

Where's member are the best ,

With a sense of belonging and have

Each other's trust.

There's only love to share ,

Everybody takes care.

Mom , Dad , Sister and Brother,

Whenever and wherever together , the home appears.

Tell Me...

Tell me the story of your hidden feelings

Tell me the story , why your wounds aren't healing.

Tell me the story of all the secrets

Which are hidden , in your heart's closet.

Tell me that , Am I also your favourite?

Beacause Now , I can't wait.

I know you're hard only from outside

Because I can see the inner you , soft and bright.

Dear Night ,

Why I have appetite

Of beautiful dreams

Wonderful and bright!

Don't be sleepless always,

Because there are so many other ways

To explore the inner me ,

And find what else could I be?

I found the most beautiful thread

Among all the relations I have

that is none other but which connects me to the person I wanna become.

"؟"

No much amount of please

is able to please you.

Doesn't matter , what you do

I can never be healed by you.

Sometimes... treated like the best , sometimes like the worst

What Do you think , Ain't I hurt ?

I'm not a toy ,

Not born , just for your Joy!

I have feelings too,

You hurt , Same can I do.

But I don't wanna be like you ,

Or else , that line would disappear that separates me from being you!

I value you , but I love my self respect

Therefore , Bye Bye.... Please forget.

The world from my window

One day , sitting in my room , I peeked out of the window...

I could see , the trees that grow..

But I was surprised, On seeing a task...

People not wearing smile, but only it's mask.

I wondered... Why's it so , why to hide which is norm?

Then someone told me.. who expresses emotions... isn't considered as strong.

I felt the depth , of that line

& questioned... Why to be an "eight" , when you're a nine.

I got another answer, People value those who have expensive watches... Not who have their precious time (for you)

I was shocked...but then I saw someone's smile....

telling to me , there's a negativity's pile.

I thought, where the opportunities could be?

I got to know that there's nothing in this world.... its just that what I wanna see.

A Lot vs Little

Do a lot , expect a little

Forgive a lot , hurt a little

Love a lot , hate a little

Help a lot , tell a little

Listen a lot , say a little

Achieve a lot , but remember a little

Give the best , expect the worst!

So that You can Improve a lot and regret a little

It's Better...

It's better to leave

when the pen becomes the reason you can't write

when the ladder becomes the reason you can't climb

when the flower becomes the reason you can't smell

when emotions become the reason you can't smile

when the name becomes the reason you can't talk

when the happiness becomes the reason you can't feel the pain....

It's always better to leave

If you...

If you forget me

I'd be speechless

Will say nothing ,

but it will hurt a lot.

Knowing that you don't know me ,

will feel like , The most precious gem I've lost.

You were always the dearest to me,

now you can't even recall , I can't even imagine how that feeling would be.

Just a span of 4 years ,

I'll either be happy or just hiding my tears.

The pain , I'll gain ,

given by the almighty.

Would hurt me a lot , If that day you'd ask

Who's Aditi?

I won't blame you , Might be my bad.

But I'll be shocked

knowing that , Those precious memories

You just forgot.

Dearest Teacher,

I always wondered , how special, important and wonderful,a teacher could be .

All these answers I found , in the thread that connects , you and me.

You don't know , let me tell you,

I thought you're a person , who always feels faded blue.

I thought you were rude ,

One who can't be emotion glued.

Until the 13th of February came,

My perspective highly changed.

I could see you , the whole opposite now

And I was like , there's so much of chao(s).

Meeting you , was one of the best experience

To learn

Getting up , after falling

Before TIME'S up.

I know that you know , but still I'll say

Coz , saying that gives me gay.

My favourite teacher... Only you are

At the top of the heart , as one of the most shining star ?.

— ADITI

Dear Grief...

Dear Grief , I love you so much

from the very bottom of my heart, which you never fail to touch.

I know that most of the people hate you ,

But I'm not someone who thinks the same as they do.

You motivate me , You Inspire me , never leave a chance,

So that I can be strong , and withstand whatever is the circumstance.

You teach me to value things , to don't get blown,

you teach me that it's ok to be alone.

You told me that I might like , all this attraction,

but being alone will tell me , what's the heart's satisfaction.

You're my teacher , you're my love,

you're the art , who makes me rise above and above.

Now , In today's world , when everybody is hating you,

I just wanna thank and give a huge hug to you.

Thank-you for all the lessons that you taught,

Thank-you for bringing the rain in my heart , where it was drought.

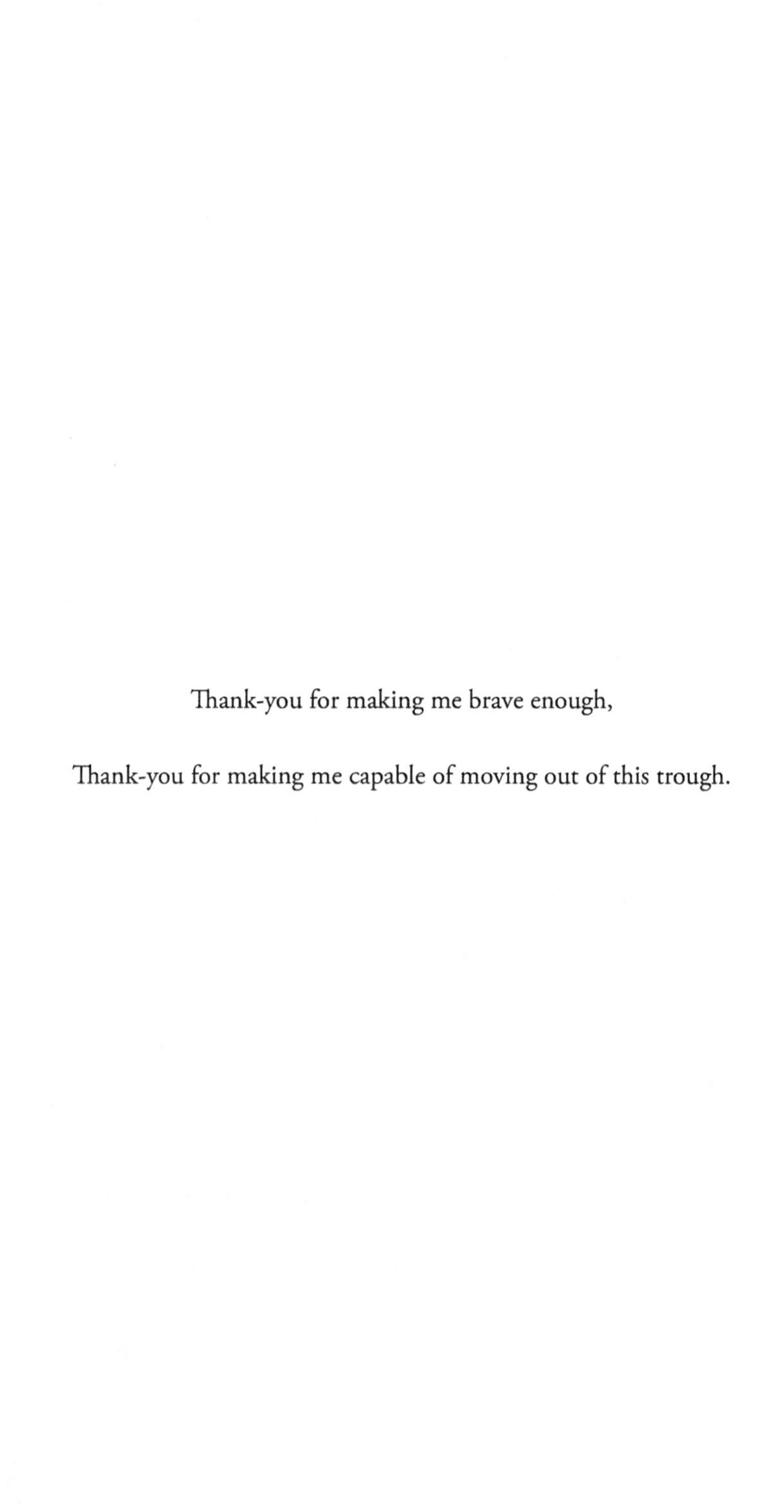

Thank-you for making me brave enough,

Thank-you for making me capable of moving out of this trough.

An elder daughter...

Being the eldest daughter... that too introvert one,

You've a lot of friends.... but still you feel alone.

You get all the new clothes ... is what People think of you,

Without thinking once.... what all happens inside you.

You're arrogant... too small to sound wise,

You'll do things... without any compromise.

Anyway... whatever they believe... it is not an easy task ,

To hide all your emotions... by wearing a fake smile's mask.

Showing that you're tension free,

While inside you is growing a responsibility's tree.

Not even ended your teen...

from inside you're also very keen.

You're the caretaker , the advisor , the counsellor ,

You are like... you weren't a child ever.

You're your sister's second mother...

for all of them... you're the secret keeper.

Responsibilities had made you... grow a little sooner,

you've sacrificed your present.... for family's better future.

I know... that you're still searching for a friend...

With whom , you can be a little childish again.

Dear Monsoon...

For me , you're one of the greatest boon!

While listening to your sound,

Calmness and peace is what I found.

Watching your drops , on that green tree,

makes me feel very free.

Along with you , comes my memories,

Oh! Days went , but I still remember those stories.

Accepting the truth

My path now is a little bit of difficult,

but the desire to walk on it, is profound.

You were a support , not too finer,

But now I've realised that I'm a tree not a climber.

Journey without you isn't that much happy ,

But now I know my actual value and my own therapy.

I knew earlier that I shouldn't be with you,

As said... Don't go where people don't value you.

But ... that love was forcing me to do so,

But now I'm happy that finally I do not follow (that love).

But remember... you're always in my heart,

and will never be apart.

I'll come surely ,

but then , I won't be feeling lonely.

And then you too will be valuing me ,

but will never get there , where you used to be (in my heart).

Hurt...

What hurts the most

is when you feel that you're lost.

Not because you failed ,

but because your friend's reality is now unveiled.

Who never wanted to be apart,

has now learnt the art.

Not like cooking or how to sing

but how to forget your bestie , or you can say how to STING.

Such experiences are really terrible ,

of course , not digestible.

you only think ,whether they've changed ,

or were they never true friends of yours ?

Who now , after meeting with new ones ,

don't remember those memories... even as blurs.

Mine or not ?

The problem is mine ,

But I'm not the solution.

Your path goes through me ,

But I'm not the destination.♥?

The job isn't mine ,

But mine is the resignation.

The stress isn't mine,

But mine is the hesitation.

The test isn't mine ,

But mine was the preparation.

The mistake wasn't mine,

Neither is the satisfaction.

I'm yours , you're mine...

Oh! I hope so , but somewhere is the opposition.

Someone else's was the intention ,

But yours was the decision.

It was not what it seems now ,

We lacked the precision.

It ended badly ,

It wasn't the intention.

Without introduction it started ,

Still is not the conclusion.

Yes I'm...

Yes I'm paying for the mistake, which I never commited.

Yes I'm playing the game, despite of

knowing the fact that I'm being cheated.

Yes I'm reading the chapter , which has been deleted.

Yes I'm wearing the sweater which never has been knitted.

Yes I'm living with the dreams , which before birth were murdered.

Yes I'm living in the world which never existed.

Yes I'm still here despite of being shifted.

Yes I'm somewhere where my existence is restricted.

Yes I'm still here where I'm not well treated.

Yes I might seem solved but I'm riddled.

Yes I'm here , where my existence is not considered.

Yes a voice is there inside me , now it can't be ignored ,

it says

Why did you come here , from where you don't belong to.

Why are you living here , where you're not supposed to.

Not committing the mistake might be the mistake ,

Who the hell cares , but the punishment is yours.

Remember...

I'm always here for you , to support you.

You don't need to say , I know you're there too.

Remember... I'm always here

With my shoulders when you're tired or need to cry.

I won't let you fall , by each of my try.

With lap , when you need to sleep.

Or if to feel lighter you just want to weep.

With all the affection , when you feel alone.

To let you be childish even if you're grown.

To heal you , when you're hurt.

With everything which you need , when you want your feelings to squirt.

To pick you up , if there's a prickle in your foot.

To make you stronger, to never let you uproot.

With my hands , to wipe your tears.

With all the requirements to let go all of your fears.

Remember I'm always here

I'm Tired Now

I promise not to cry , tears wiped the glow.

Scar is still on the face , things got blewed which I never wanted to blow.

Tears wiped all the beautiful moments , horrible ones are still there.

Tried a lot to forget ... forgot all the goods , bads are still here.

Tried to clean my mind ,

but the dust got refined.

Broom removed all the decor , stains last yet.

Could've removed the dust , unfortunately it was wet.

Tried to clean , but damaged the precious wall.

Which I never wanted , It let that thing fall.

Used to speak less , was misunderstood.

Started to speak , again not understood.

Now tired of saying , spoke a lot.

Let silence prevail now , don't care if it is not got.

Was changing I guess , yes you made me realise.

I'm thankful to you , Now I won't , even if you criticise.

Stubborn and questioning to obeying and accepting.

Was it good ? Don't know.

But if you can't , then I shouldn't is just what I know.

While trying to erase the wound.

I erased the glow

Wound is still here , those reason of smile got blown.

While trying to forget some memories , I missed making some as well.

Their pain still hurts , Those some good ones , didn't last as well.

It's About You...

Your sweet words , when I'm hurt.

Your cute actions , to remove my face's dirt.

The way you hug , to make me feel secure.

Your terrible jokes , to help me cure.

The way you make me listen your heartbeat.

Holding me tight in your arms , in the empty street.

Your kisses on my forehead, to make me relax.

Your being with me , yes it seems like time lapse.

Your care for me , to help me stand calmly.

Your efforts to join my broken pieces beautifully.

Just Don't

Don't hug me , your clothes will get wet.

Don't want to say , no argument no bet.

Don't come near me , unnecessarily you would be shouted.

I'm fine alone , let not this place get crowded.

Don't talk to me , you'll get hurt.

You'll get only dirty , as I'm a dessert.

Don't try to heal my wound , you'd mess up your hand.

Blood won't stop , not only with blood but you'd be messed up as well as with sand.

Don't try to clean my stains , you'd be covered with dust.

Just leave me here , and go somewhere find your lust.

Don't prioritize me , I don't deserve.

For someone deserving , please preserve.

Don't chase me , you'll get a thorn in your foot.

No , it too won't work , don't give the excuse of wearing a boot.

The Day...

The day I'd convience myself that there's nothing to lose or gain ,

Is the day I'd be happy again.

The day I'd stop being tough ,

Is the day I'd cherish all the love.

The day I'd be able to say my things ,

Is the day I'd start feeling lighter and would fly with my wings.

The day I'd be able to speak the inner me ,

Is the day when I'd feel too free.

The day I'd know life's different gears ,

Is the day I wouldn't be left with any of my tears.

The day I'd find the lost me,

Is the day my heart would smile I guarantee.

Waiting for that day to stop the succumb ,

Either I've to find alone or the person hasn't yet come.

You..

While watching you come closer,

My heart aligns it's rhythm to compose the best song ever.

While feeling your touch,

my skin softens itself

more than a soapstone.

While imagining you,

My thoughts roam

below the Challenger Deep.

While talking to you,

time slips at a rate

faster than blazar jet.

While being with you,

The amount of love seems

more than the capacity of this ever expanding universe.

Your Eye's Ocean

Deep down into the ocean of your eyes, I've dived.

You're one of the reason without which,

I would have just survived.

A garden too green, with beautiful and colourful flowers.

Come into the garden, you'll grow by my love's showers.

The sun shining bright, becomes just null.

When you smile,

even the star seems dull.

Clouds in the sky, and the sky turning dark.

Leaves leaving the branches of the tree and

it's wet bright brown bark.

Droplets of water gently touching the ground,

You and me and no one to surround.

The wind cold enough to make me shiver,

And your arms to wrap around there.

When your hand will pass through the bushes of my hair,

Then your one hand on my waist and one through my hair coming to the

cheeks.

My eyes in your eyes, measuring the depth of your eye's ocean.

Thunder in the sky , a shiny yet dull light.

Enough bright to glow well, but much lesser than your smile.

3. Chapter 3: The Hindi Ones...

All the poems now are written in Hindi :)

अब तो कराहने दे....

वादों भरोसों कसमों को आज फिर टूट जाने दो

उम्मीदों से टूट कर आज मुझे फिर बिखर जाने दो

अरसों बाद मिला जो आज फिर बिछड़ जाने दो

अपने अंदर की आग में अब खुद ही जल जाने दो

हदों की जो लकीरें हैं आज उनसे फिर गुज़र जाने दो

बस बहुत हुआ , इस दर्द से अब तो कराहने दो

सहेज कर रखा था अबतक जो , अब उसे खो जाने दो

ख्वाब पूरे ना हो पाएं उससे पहले ही एक दफा फिर टूट जाने दो

अंदर की वो आवाज़ जो हमेशा हारी आज उसे जीत जाने दो

अबतक अंदर जो तड़प रही थी आज उसे मर जाने दो

जोड़ हुए टुकड़ों को आज फिर बिखर जाने दो

बस बहुत हुआ इस दर्द से अब तो कराहने दो

ख्वाहिशें जो जगी थीं आज उन्हें मर जाने दो

मुकम्मल नहीं जो किस्मत को , उसे अब भूल जाने दो

नजदीकियां बहुत एहसास की अब फासलों को बढ़ जाने दो

अच्छी थी वो यादें पर अब उसने पर हो जाने दो।

कह लिया बहुत अब खामोशियों को अपना राज ढाहने दो।

अगली सुबह ना देख पाए अब इसे रात ही रह जाने दो।

बस बहुत हुआ इस दर्द से अब तो कराहने दो।

Han ya Nahi ?

प्यास अब बुझ गई , या पानी अब बचा नहीं।

रोना अब आता नहीं, या रो रो के आँखें ये सूख गईं।

मुस्कुराना अब भूल गई , या मुस्कुराना चाहती नहीं।

समझने वाला कोई मिला नहीं, या किसी को समझा समझा के थक गई।

ज़िंदगी से अब गिला नहीं, या शिकायतें कर कर के थक गई।

दिल अब दुखता नहीं, या दर्द को अब छुपाना सीख गई ।

चलना अब चाहती नहीं, या छालों से रुक गई।

खुशियाँ तुझे रास नहीं या उनकी तलाश में थक गई।

पूछना अब चाहती नहीं या पूछ पूछ के थक गई।

अब और टुकड़े नहीं हो सकते भला इस कदर क्या टूट गई।

शब्द खत्म हो गए या उनकी तलाश में भटक गई ।

कुछ नहीं खोती अब या खोने को कुछ बचा नहीं।

उम्मीद अब करती नहीं या उम्मीदों से ही टूटी तू।

गलतियों का एहसास नहीं या गलतियाँ अब तक न भूली तू।

स्ट्रॉन्ग है अब बहुत या और कमज़ोर नहीं पड़ सकती तू।

बोल ना आज यहीं क्यों रुक गई ,

शब्द अब खत्म हो गए या उनकी तलाश में भटक गई ?

कोशिशि तू अपनी जारी रख

इस विशाल दुनिया में, मोह माया के इस जाल में

कोशिशि तू अपनी जारी रख

ना मिले कोई वजह खुश होने की...

तो बेवजह खुश होने की आदत रख

ना कोई अपना है, ना कोई पराया है,

सबको क्षमा करके तू आगे बढ़ने की कोशिशि रख।

आकाश से ऊंची सीमा है तेरी, तू हौसलों को बुलंद रख

मंजिल स्वयं चलकर तेरे पास आएगी, तू कोशिशि अपनी जारी रख।

समय को यूं व्यर्थ न कर, जुनून को तू जिंदा रख

मंजिल की फिक्र छोड, पथ का आनंद जारी रख

दूसरों को खुश करने की ख्वाहिशि त्याग, दुखी ना करने का प्रयत्न जारी रख

संसार ना होगा कभी तुझसे खुश, खुद हार ना मानने का साहस रख।

बुरा वक्त है बीत जाएगा, लगाया है वृक्ष तो फल अवश्य आएगा

खुद को ना यूं मायूस कर, थोडा सा तो धीरज रख।

कभी भी तू घमंड ना कर, दुनिया जल जाएगी तेरी सफलता से ही

बस याद रख एक बात परिंदे, उम्मीद तेरी ये टूटे ना कभी।

मार्गदर्शन

For my teacher...

कैसे करूं मैं आपका शुक्रियादा

नहीं है इतनी इन शब्दों की मर्यादा

सख्ती से तो कभी नर्मी से बताया

सदा एव सही मार्गदर्शन कराया

कर देना माफ़ मुझे अगर हो सके तो

जैसा चाहा आपने, वैसी पाई ना बन तो

माफ़ करना गर जो कभी हो सताया

हमेशा सही मार्गदर्शन कराया

साल भर बाद मैं ना रहूंगी यहां पर

याद आएंगे साथ बिताए वो हर पल

चाहा था पर वो समय ना रुक पाया

सदा एव सही मार्गदर्शन कराया

जाते जाते मैं बस इतना कहूंगी

आपकी जगह ना मैं किसी को से सकूंगी

काबू करना कोह पर आपने सिखाया

हमेशा सही मार्गदर्शन कराया।

Thankyou so much for coming to here. Hope you had a good experience.